I WILL Remember YOU

WORDS OF LIFE, LOVE AND GRATITUDE

Alecia Smith Mueller

20 Twenty
Literary Group

ISBN
978-1-962868-62-4 (Paperback)
978-1-962868-63-1 (eBook)
978-1-962868-61-7 (Hardcover)

This book is my gift to you. It expresses my deep gratitude and affection for what you have meant in my life!

This dedication is

for: _____

Who is my guiding light.

I WILL *Remember* YOU

I see you there

As you have lately been,

A Pharos, uplifting and steadfast,

A beacon in my life.

Your nature is constant, faithful,

As selfless as you are true.

The gentleness of your light

Belies its power to heal.

Remember always that

You truly are a guiding light.

I give thanks for you,

Dear One,

And I will always remember.

I am just a lonely traveler:

A courageous ship,

But one of many,

Sailing through time and space.

Alecia Smith Mueller

The ocean of my existence is

Often deeper than

My understanding.

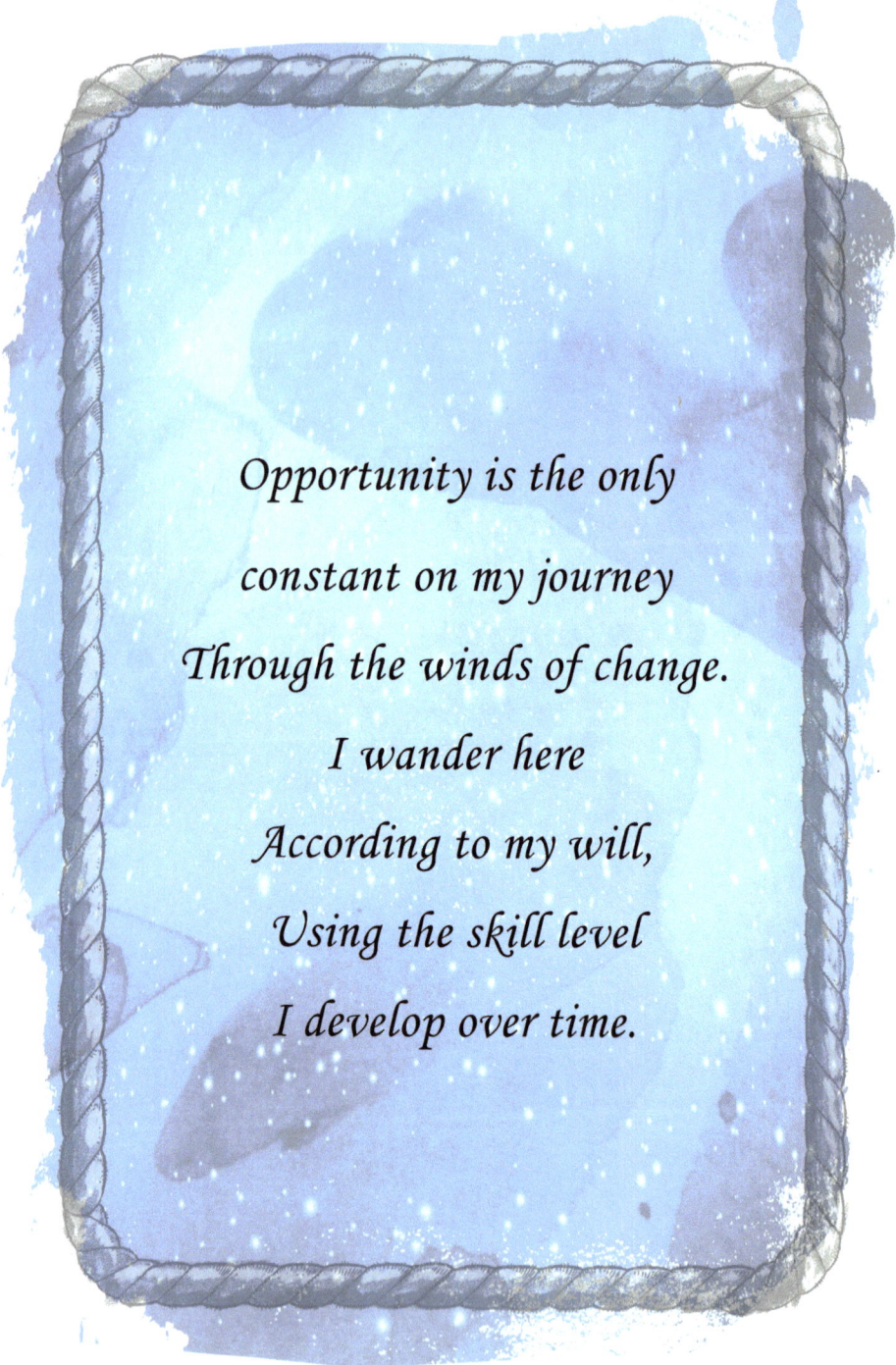

Opportunity is the only

constant on my journey

Through the winds of change.

I wander here

According to my will,

Using the skill level

I develop over time.

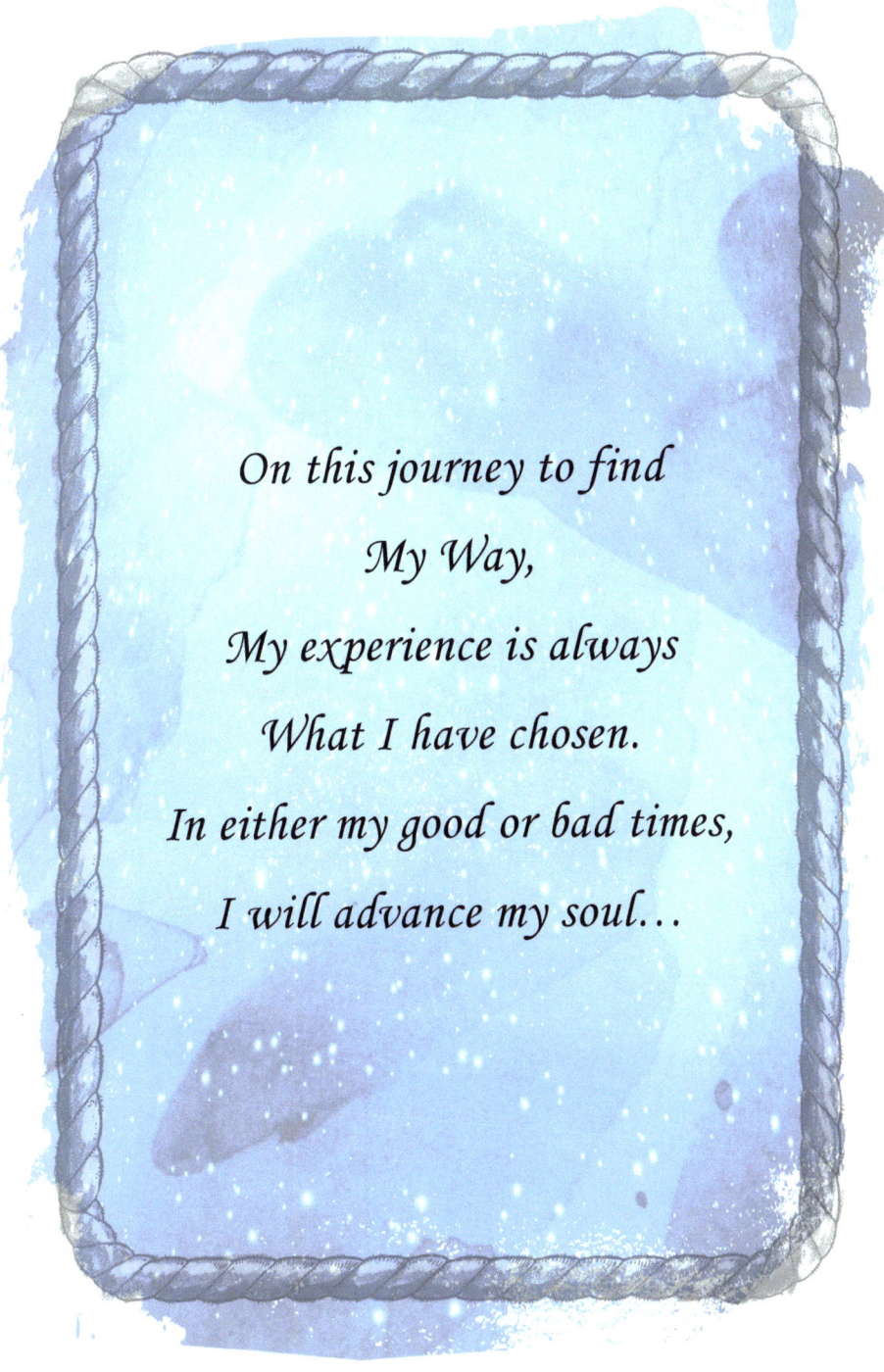

On this journey to find

My Way,

My experience is always

What I have chosen.

In either my good or bad times,

I will advance my soul…

For surely nothing
That is good and true
Is ever lost.

Alecia Smith Mueller

I am aware this ship
Has been entrusted to me
And I know
I AM the captain.

Memory is my ship's log

Where I write the answers

To life's questions:

"Where am I going?"

"Where have I been?"

And the best one,

"Where am I now?"

When my mortal memories fade,

As they surely will,

I shall be comforted in knowing

That all is added

And nothing is taken away

In the Book of Life.

Faith, hope and love
Are my compass, my rudder,
And my anchor
As I travel through life.

With the choices I make
I hope to keep this ship
Upright and safe.
The weather I face is
perceived as either
Friend or foe
By the pound of flesh
Who is the only me I know.

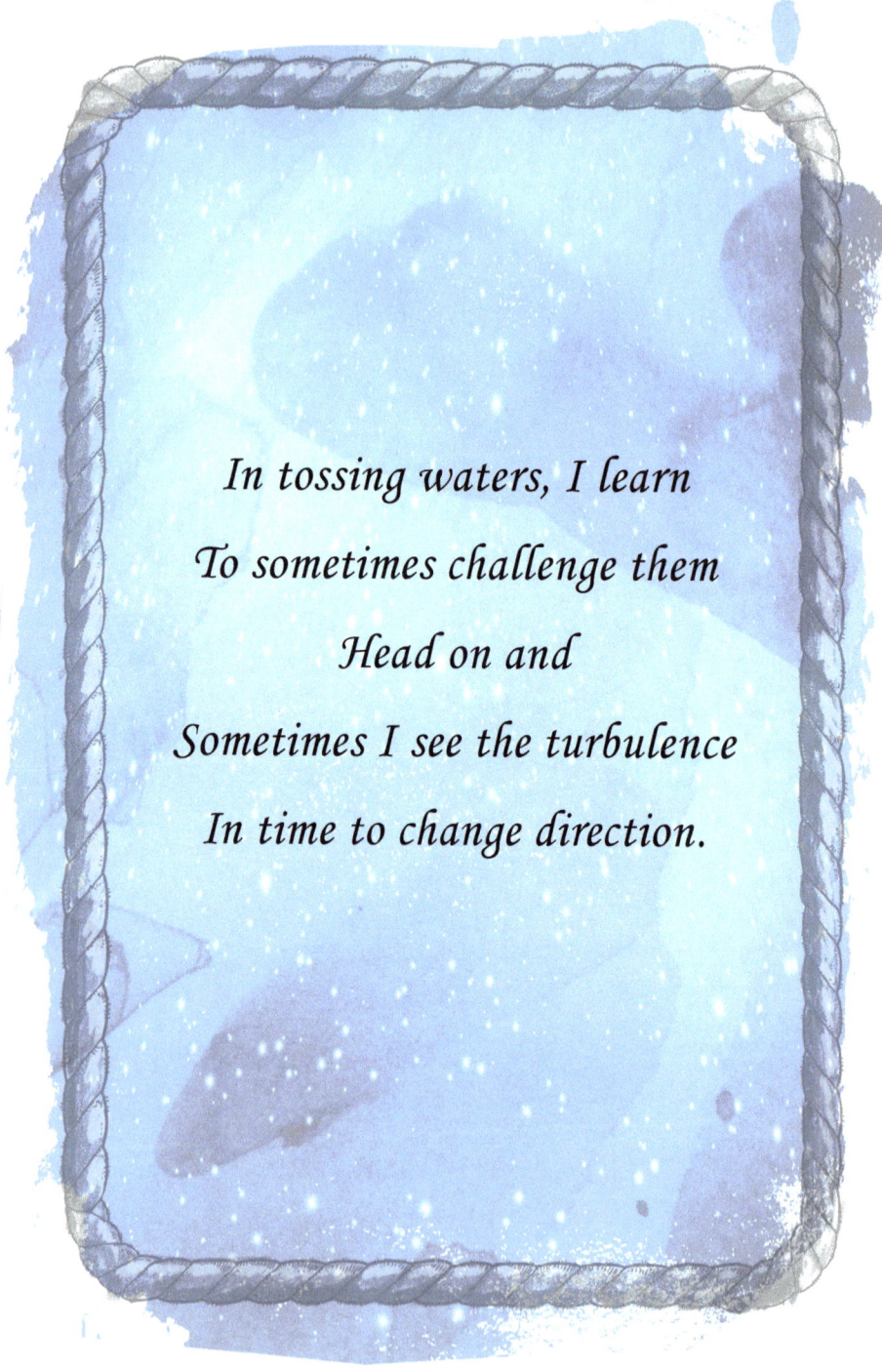

In tossing waters, I learn
To sometimes challenge them
Head on and
Sometimes I see the turbulence
In time to change direction.

14   *Alecia Smith Mueller*

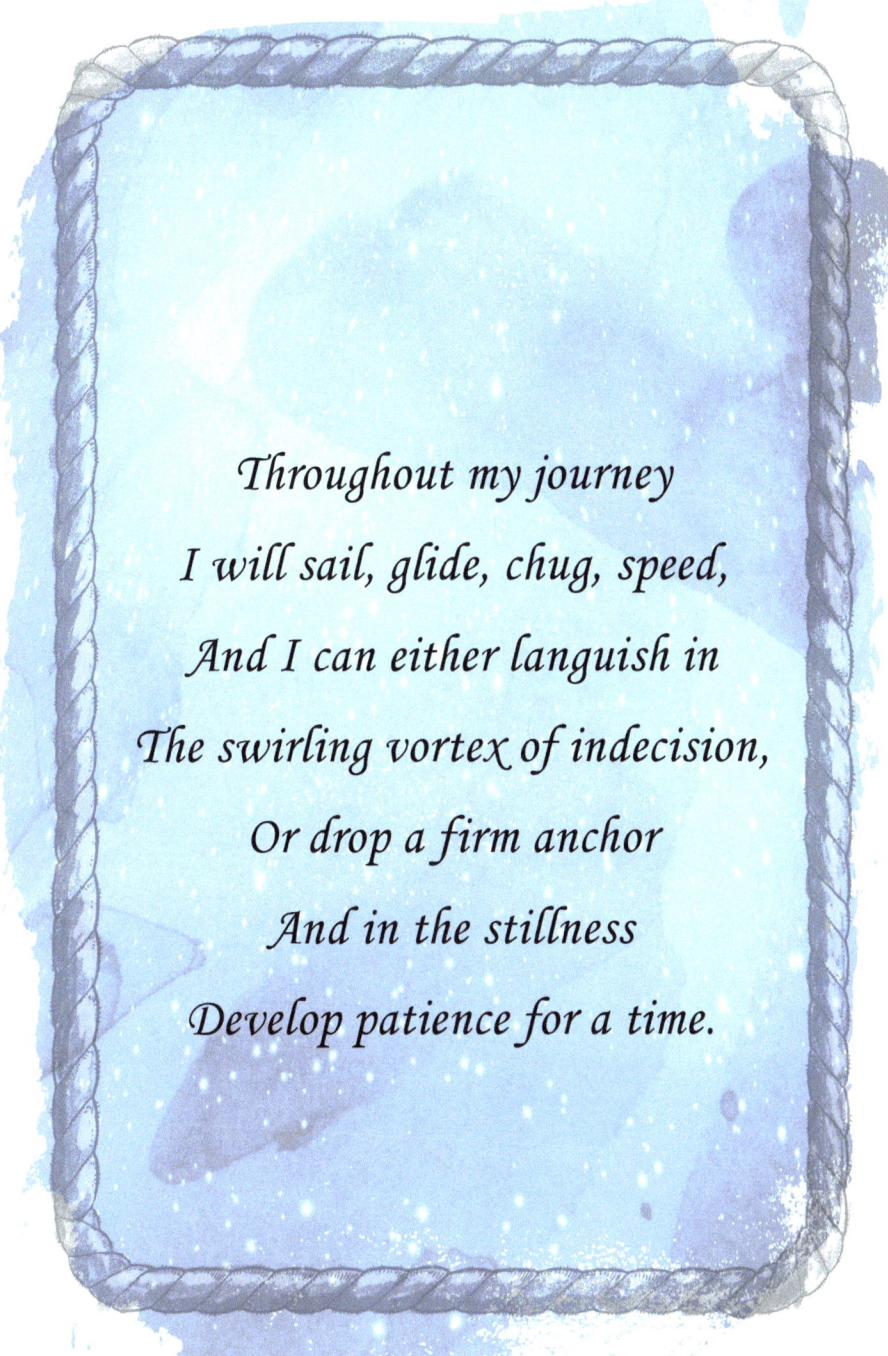

Throughout my journey
I will sail, glide, chug, speed,
And I can either languish in
The swirling vortex of indecision,
Or drop a firm anchor
And in the stillness
Develop patience for a time.

Danger allows that I may
Succumb to the abyss
Or be rent on the shoals,
In the ravages of a storm.
In troubled waters, many times
My soul searches for guidance.

But whenever clouds threaten,
Or the fog rolls in,
I have learned that if I have
Faith enough to expect it,
A lighthouse will appear.

You are that lighthouse.

Knowing you are there

Gives me peace

And calms my fears.

Alecia Smith Mueller

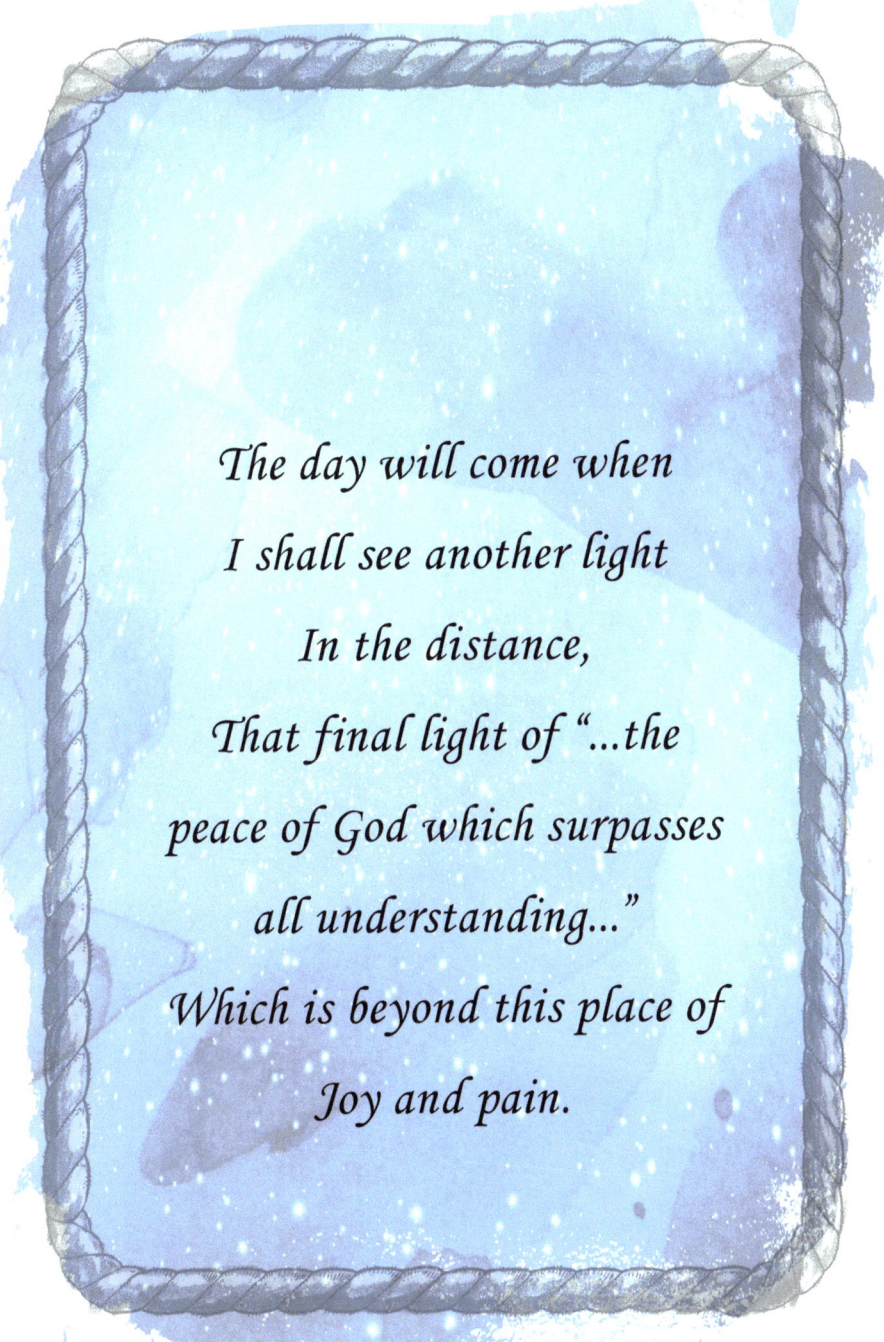

The day will come when
I shall see another light
In the distance,
That final light of "...the
peace of God which surpasses
all understanding..."
Which is beyond this place of
Joy and pain.

And when the spark of life is

Finally extinguished

Within my broken ship,

I will know that beacon is

The light of Hope and Home.

There I will find a better place

To grant an ending to this

Journey of a storm-tossed soul.

Then, from the comfort of

The Hereafter,

My enduring memory

Will joyfully recall

Your love-light.

And steady and true,

With me,

Forever it will shine.

With affection,

from : _____

www.ingramcontent.com/pod-product-compliance
Lightning Source LLC
Chambersburg PA
CBHW040849120626
46547CB00001B/98